Encouraged & Ignited

SETTING THE POWER OF PRAYER ABLAZE IN YOUR LIFE

Cristy Frazier

Copyright © 2024 Cristy Frazier

All rights reserved. No part of this publication may be reproduced, distributed, or transmitted in any form or by any means, including photocopying, recording, or other electronic or mechanical methods, without the publisher's prior written permission. In accordance with the U. S. Copyright Act of 1976, the scanning, uploading, and electronic sharing of any part of this book without the permission of the author is unlawful piracy and theft of the author's intellectual property. If you would like to use material from this book, prior written permission must be obtained.

Unless otherwise noted, all scriptures referenced are from the ESV (English Standard Version). The ESV® Bible (The Holy Bible, English Standard Version®). ESV® Text Edition: 2016. Copyright © 2001 by Crossway, a publishing ministry of Good News Publishers. The ESV® text has been reproduced in cooperation with and by permission of Good News Publishers. Unauthorized reproduction of this publication is prohibited. All rights reserved.

Holman Christian Standard Bible®
Copyright © 1999, 2000, 2002, 2003, 2009 by Holman Bible Publishers.
Used with permission by Holman Bible Publishers, Nashville, Tennessee. All rights reserved.

Geneva Bible, 1599 Edition. Published by Tolle Lege Press. All rights reserved. No part of the publication may be reproduced or transmitted in any form or by any means, electronic or mechanical, without written permission from the publisher, except in the case of brief quotations in articles, reviews, and broadcasts.

The author has made every effort to check and ensure the accuracy of the information presented in this book. However, the information herein is sold without a warranty, either expressed or implied. Neither the author, illustrator, publisher, nor any deal or distributor of this book will be held liable for any damages caused either directly or indirectly by the instructions and information contained in this book.

The events, places, and conversations in this book have been recreated from memory. The chronology of some events has been compressed. When necessary, the names and identifying characteristics of individuals and places have been changed to maintain anonymity.

For permission requests, write to the publisher, addressed "Attention: Permissions Coordinator," at the address below or via email at thescarletrosepublishing@gmail.com.

Cover Design: Peyton Richmond & Savanna Callis
Illustrations: Mallory Humphries
Typographer: Eli Creasy
Scarlet Rose Publishing; thescarletrosepublishing@gmail.com; PO BOX 922, White House, TN 37188
Author: Cristy Frazier; cristyfrazier.com

"Your prayers author your tomorrow"

Cristy Frazier

Encouraged & Ignited

Table of Contents

	Welcome	1
1.	The Spark That Started It All	5
2.	The Power of Prayer Realized	10
3.	A Call to Prayer	13
4.	Always Start with a Clean Slate	15
5.	We, as Followers of the Way, are Instructed to Pray	20
6.	Lord, Teach Us to Pray	22
7.	Avenues of Prayer	24
8.	Prayer Examples of the Bible	29
9.	My Foundational Prayers	34
10.	Jesus and Prayer	43
11.	The Words of Your Mouth Declare Your Destiny	49
12.	Why Am I Not Seeing My Prayers Answered?	54
13.	Biblical Examples of Firstfruits	56
14.	In the Days Ahead	59
15.	There Are No Accidents in the Kingdom of God	61
16.	Until Next Time	66
	Appendix A: Prayer Survey	68
	Appendix B: An Invitation	71
	Appendix C: Behind the Scenes	80
	Acknowledgments	82
	About the Author	84
	Like What You've Read?	86
	Notes	88

Welcome

Hello! I sincerely thank you for your interest and support in your purchase. I want you to know that I am grateful to you even if you never make it beyond this page. I have prayed for you and every person who would lay hands upon these pages. May God richly bless you beyond measure.

What you can expect as you read through the pages ahead are my ramblings on prayer. If you know me, you are neither shocked nor taken by surprise. And, thanks to my mom and daughters, I have the t-shirt to prove it. It reads: "Prayer is my hobby." My hope and prayer for each person who picks up this book is that they, too, will fall in love with prayer, enrich their current prayer time, and ultimately, be encouraged to pray without ceasing. Pray, Give Thanks, and Rejoice in "all" circumstances (1 Thessalonians 5:16-18). Prayers are powerful. They are not just words but utterances of the soul that open the heart of the Father and unleash the resources of Heaven to us here below.

> Rejoice always, pray without ceasing, give thanks in all circumstances; for this is the will of God in Christ Jesus for you.
> *1 Thessalonians 5:16-18*

Whether you are a newbie or a seasoned veteran of prayer, I genuinely think of this book as a rallying of the troops to understand *why* to pray while providing practical applications on *how*. I will give biblical examples of prayer and avenues of prayer the Bible commissions us to pray for ourselves and others. Wherever you find yourself in your prayer life, I am confident you will walk away with an "ah-ha" moment along the way.

As you read along, you will find a common thread of how prayer was a catalyst for my life to be reborn. Those prayers have directed me and woven my life into the fabric of others' lives, leading me to this moment I am living here with you. Every moment, prayer, and person have led you and me here together. I am now woven into the fabric of your life, and you are woven into mine. It is the tapestry of the kingdom of God. Can you picture it? I bet it is beautiful from Heaven's point of view. I look forward to seeing it one day and witnessing how each thread was personally hand-stitched by a very loving and intentional Father.

The Lord has raised me in him through prayer and on bended knees over the last ten years. He has taught, corrected, comforted, and encouraged me through the hours of prayer spent before him. I know without a doubt that I would not be alive, married, or the person I am today without the power of prayer. Prayer is effective. Prayer is alive. Prayer builds up, and prayer destroys evil altars and strongholds. Prayer is a mighty roar and a whisper. I love prayer! Prayer is my passion. Prayer is the fire that fuels my days.

What each prayer prayed, each tear cried, and each groaning proceeding from my lips implanted within me over the last ten years is now being birthed and brought forth here through my writings. What will God birth through your time in prayer with him? What seeds within you are just waiting to be watered by the tears of your confessions, repentance, and forgiveness in prayer? With each prayer prayed and tear that hit the ground, I became the woman, wife, and mom I always wanted to be. I was transformed by his teaching, love, and guidance in those tender, vulnerable moments before him at all hours of the day and night. The great thing about God is that there is no end to the evolution of our being. We are forever being transformed into the image of Christ.

May the turn of each page ahead foster a boldness in prayer unlike anything you have ever experienced. May those who did not previously have a heart for prayer be encouraged to pray and understand the power of prayer after this journey.

What you will experience as you journey ahead with me may very well differ from other books you have read. This book is more conversational—as if you and I are friends sitting together and discussing our lives and prayer. We may be on the sofa, you at one end and me at the other. We each have a cup of our favorite beverage and freshly baked cookies that are still warm and gooey in our hands. I *love* fresh-baked chocolate chip cookies—even white chocolate macadamia nut will do. Those are my *favorites!*

I would be sitting with my feet up on the sofa, my hair pulled back in a clip, and wearing oversized, baggy clothes because I am way more concerned with comfort than looks (this is precisely how I am now as I write this for you). I would offer you a cozy blanket—even if it is 100 degrees outside—because that is always considered cozy in my world. I would pull back the curtain and share tidbits of how I experienced a total mindset and lifestyle change regarding prayer, and I would bring you along behind the scenes of the evolution of this book. Why? Because I love hearing the hows and whys. If we were sitting together and chatting, I would not just want to hear the big cover story of your life but also what led to that story and what happened after the end of the book.

For more on my writing journey, please visit Appendix C: Behind the Scenes. I want you to see that every word, prayer, and even the title and timing of this book are all in God's hands. It's wild to think that it all originates from a simple prayer prayed over me as a child. That spark started the fire for prayer that now burns within me.

Grab your snuggly blanket and let the conversation roll...

1

THE SPARK THAT STARTED IT ALL

This story begins with a praying father and ends with a display of how amazing it is that God worked through ten years of human interactions to wrap this book up with his divine bow. You will see that life with God is amazing, and he wastes absolutely nothing!

The pivotal moment in my life—one of those "stone markers" regarding prayer—was when I was between three and four years old. It was a beautiful, sunny day. All was well with the world in my innocent eyes. I was enjoying time with my father, which was rare due to my parents having gone through a divorce when I was two. At this time, I was only able to see my father every other weekend per their custody agreement. Unbeknownst to that little me at the time, those car rides with my father would be my only time alone with him for the rest of our days together.

I enjoyed my time with my father. We would spend most of our car rides singing. He had a good singing voice, but we both loved to sing. Growing up, those moments riding in the car with my father were the only time I felt like I had a father. I felt like I was a part of something bigger and more natural. Something like a real family. Sadly, I do not recall experiencing that feeling with him outside of those car rides.

On this particular day, he was driving down the main thoroughfare, Quintard Avenue, in Anniston, Alabama. I was sitting in the passenger seat, perched on my knees, and not wearing a seatbelt—at that time, seatbelts weren't even legally required.

The driver of the truck in front of us abruptly slammed on the brakes, which in turn led my father to slam on his brakes, which thrust my big mouth right into the dash! As I peeled my lips from the dash, blood immediately and profusely gushed from my mouth. My mouth blew up like a balloon. My father didn't waste a minute! He pulled over, walked around to my side of the car, opened the door, knelt, and began praying over me. The blood ceased its gushing, and all was well.

That, my reader friends, was the moment Heaven invaded my life in a very real, tangible, and significant way that I have *never* forgotten. It made a considerable impact that lit the pilot light of prayer within me, which continues to be fanned and strengthened today. I hope it never gets old and, like a wildflower, never stops multiplying.

As you can imagine, I learned the power of prayer from my father's example. With endless weapons of warfare waged against our relationship, his prayers were what I valued most. I knew the atmosphere would change and the mountains would be moved if I called my father and he started praying. My father continued to build upon this example of prayer until he transitioned into eternity.

Once my father passed on, an already tumultuous life was then shattered in many ways. In my mind, far beyond repair. Quickly, I realized as the days rolled on, I could no longer call my daddy for prayer. That left me feeling hopeless and weary. I had never really known of others who could pray and have all of Heaven's attention. I wasn't even sure if other such people existed anywhere around me. It was rare that I saw hope, faith, and miraculous signs and wonders like when my daddy would pray.

Losing my father was very difficult for me. There were many feelings that we would never have an opportunity to resolve. Many conversations we would never get to have. There was no opportunity to make memories and make up for years of lost time and bonding outside of our car rides. I not only lost my father, but I also lost most of my connection to that side of my family.

My grandfather, grandmother, and cousin all passed within a couple of years.

My whole world seemed to be falling apart. My marriage had already started crumbling because of my deep sadness. I began to see myself as a burden to my husband and children. I was anxious. I was depressed. I was at rock bottom. Death seemed to be my only way out! For years, it was all I thought about from the moment I woke up until I went to bed and tried to sleep. I had lost so much that I did not want to go on. I felt like my family would be better off without me. I did not want to live in a sea of pain for another day. I did not want to be miserable, and I did not want to make my husband and children miserable either.

So, I did the only thing I knew to do: pray. I started praying for God to send me a praying warrior like my father. I would see my husband off to work, take our daughters to school, and then come home and dissolve into a puddle of tears on the floor. I was in utter pain. This had become a new reality for me due to unhealthy emotions permeating my body 24/7. I would cry out to God to save me or take me. Then, the answer to my prayers moved into the house across the street. Christine.

She had a daughter the same age as our youngest. They became friends, and both were a part of the same cheerleading team. My husband and I began attending a Bible study that Christine and her husband led in their home. Our families began to hang out together. She and I started walking around the neighborhood or the local park together occasionally. We talked about life as we walked, and she shared her testimony with me. She shared stories of her time in prayer with prayer groups back where they had moved from. Something about her testimony and these miraculous stories started stirring something in me. Something like I had not felt since I heard my father pray or heard his testimonies of the moves of God when he prayed with people.

As an adult, I was at church whenever the doors opened. I was very involved in church activities. My husband and I co-led a youth group. I participated in the women's ministry. I organized supper club and bunko gatherings. I was around church people all the time. However, I rarely saw this hope, faith, and miraculous signs and wonders like when my father would pray.

I quickly realized there was something different in Christine than all the other "church folks" I knew. One thing became evident: this woman prayed with passion and purpose. She prayed with power and the reality that her prayers would be answered. This confidence and boldness were like nothing I had seen in anyone I had ever known but my father. When she prayed, I knew Heaven listened and took notice. It was as if I could feel her prayers. Her prayers were not empty words. They were electric and ignited. I wanted to know more!

One day, I got the nerve to ask her to pray for me after our Bible study. She did, and my life was shaken from top to bottom and everywhere in between. Nothing, and I do mean *nothing*, has been the same since! A passion for prayer was ignited in my life. That pilot light that my father lit in me as a little girl suddenly burst into flames. Christine had just provided the fuel for the fire.

Did everything become perfect in my life that day? No. However, the power of God became clear in my life. Chains were loosed. Healing began. Freedom suddenly appeared attainable. Truth and hope began to arise and come alive within me. Unlike anything I had felt before, I immediately experienced a joyful hope and expectation of good to come. It was as if confidence and hope passed from her to me through her laying her hands upon me and praying for me. I felt God had heard my cry for help and sent Christine as my lifeline. I am forever changed and forever a fierce advocate for prayer. I live in a new reality of the mighty power of prayer.

I haven't stopped praying since she prayed for me that day and never will. I believe in and encourage prayer. It is one of the most powerful tools in our spiritual tool belt. We can change directions, timelines, bloodlines, and atmospheres all over the planet just by having a little chat with Jesus.

As life seems to go at times, God quickly shifted me and Christine and led us in different directions. Shortly after this pivotal, life-changing moment, God moved me and my family out of state. It was as if God said, *Okay, you've learned what I need you to here. It's time to go and share that newfound knowledge over here with this new group of people. It is time to allow them to share what I have been doing in their lives with you.*

Even though life no longer has Christine and me running in the same circles, I pray that she is and forever will be blessed beyond measure. Because of her care and enthusiasm for prayer, I know I am blessed, and I hope you will be, too.

2

The Power of Prayer Realized

My journey of a *personal* prayer life started with an audience of one: me. The Lord taught me and walked me through ten years of praying while sitting before him. It was as if the Lord took me by the hand and led me into his classroom.

First, he began to deconstruct my understanding of prayer. Then, he started reconstructing new foundations based on the Word and the knowledge I gleaned by the leading of the Spirit.

In my life, the prayers of others make up pieces of the blueprint, giving me a foundation and vocabulary to build upon while I create my own intimate prayer life as I enter his presence at the foot of his throne.

The goal for everyone as they progress through these pages is to give each of you a foundation of biblical truths regarding prayer to stand on. Communing and communicating with your Heavenly Father through the avenue of prayer allows us the opportunity to encounter his presence.

I will warn you upfront that the enemies of your heart will try to distract you with the worries of life so that you may never discover this powerful spiritual weapon. May the information within ignite a fire that jump-starts or reignites your prayer life. May the Holy Spirit prick your heart to take your needs, your marriage, your city, your country, and your whatever to your Heavenly Father in prayer.

If you have never prayed or had a dedicated prayer life, may the words within these pages ignite a desire for you to begin to pray. If you struggle to pray or are not familiar with the power of prayer, I hope this book will highlight ways you can begin incorporating prayer into your everyday life and ultimately see God's power through the utterances of those prayers.

If you are reading these pages, are familiar with prayer, and have consistent prayer time, may these words reinforce its value so that you never make light of those prayers or question their significance again.

Whether anyone else reads these words or gets anything from their penning, I know the life-changing effect each word has had on my life and those around me. Over the years, I have witnessed how my life, which has been transformed by prayer, has inspired others around me to pray and inquire to learn more about prayer. My life transformation has brought reconciliation and peace in my closest relationships—some of which I never thought would experience healing. While I am honored and touched when others request my prayers, I am deeply moved when I hear others pray or learn of others praying who did not previously have confidence in prayer, much less a prayer life of their own.

My life has been spared and renewed by prayer. My marriage has been redeemed. What a blessing for my children! I am forever changed, and so is my bloodline. I stand in confident assurance of this.

As you journey through these pages, my heart is that you will be encouraged to pray without ceasing. May you, too, have pages of testimonies to come. Testimonies regarding your own life and those who watch the evolution and transformation from your growing prayer life and are ignited to begin their own.

My prayer for you as you journey through this book:

> *Father God, please block out the noise and distractions for each reader as they journey through this book. Please mute the mouth of the enemy over the one who holds this book. Please open the heart, mind, and soul of each reader to receive all that you have awaiting them. Please seal tightly all that you do within them along the way so that it cannot be robbed from them nor tainted by their flesh or the works of the enemy. Please draw each reader to your bosom. May readers enjoy the safety of opening their hearts to you, asking the hard questions, and praying boldly, resulting in all of hell trembling. May each reader be encouraged and ignited to visit their knees often and emboldened to pray for the rest of their days. May their prayer life abound in fullness and their soul find rest and peace as they sit in your presence. In Jesus's name, amen!*

3

A Call to Prayer

This book is a call to prayer. While prayer is not meant to be complicated, I have found that many people truly believe it is, and the unknowns keep them from attempting. With God's prompting, I felt a strong desire to take what I had learned over the years and share it with you in this book. I have seen and read many books of prayers, but I have never read one like the one you are about to read. After years in the church and praying among many prayer groups, it became apparent that most of us had no clear path through prayer and no understanding deeper than praying for ourselves and those under our roof.

This was confirmed for me a few years ago after my husband and I felt drawn to open our home and start a small group with members from our local fellowship. During those first few weeks of meeting, it was evident rather quickly that while many had been in the fellowship of believers since the womb, they did not have a personal prayer life of their own. The majority did not even know they could sit and listen to God rather than throwing up a "Hail Mary" prayer like one would throw a Hail Mary pass out of desperation during a football game. This understanding was one that my husband and I both had wrestled with only a few years prior. Neither he nor I grew up with any understanding that God wanted a personal relationship with his children.

Such ideas were taught to be nonsense by most and even heresy by others. It was our understanding that relationship and interaction with God the Father was only for the afterlife. Nothing to see and experience here! Keep moving!

Seeing the same wrestling among the members of our small group confirmed that prayer is not taught in most churches and, therefore, not *caught* because the other items on the schedule typically take more precedence than modeling prayer and leading the flock into intimate prayer time. For that reason, my heart was even more drawn to developing a resource in the hope that they may begin to ponder the *what-ifs* of an intimate prayer life of their own.

God has been fanning the flame of the importance of prayer in my life for years, and what we experienced in our small group was just another occurrence of God blowing on that flame. It is as if God kept pointing to prayer for my own life and stressing the importance that what I was learning was not meant just for me but for all God's children. An intimate personal relationship with him is what he longs for all to seek and find.

I feel I am amid a cathartic process of taking all that I have learned through those years of sitting in his classroom, compiling it, only to hand it back to him through my obedience to his call to write this book. I would have never dreamed of writing this without those precious moments spent with him. I think this is what God wants for us all. He wants us to gather around him and allow him to speak to each of us and teach us the way we should go instead of always leaning on the studying and reasoning of others. There is a time and place to glean from the fields of another, but at some point, you must plant and harvest from your own.

4

Always Start with a Clean Slate

Early on in learning about prayer, I was taught that before I petition the Father for anything—particularly for myself and my family—I need to check my heart. Is there anything I need to repent of, anyone I need to forgive, or anyone I need to apologize to? It is always best to begin with a clean slate! Considering that warrior tip, I have included a prayer my husband, Chet, wrote below. It represents the humility and reverence we need to embody before we dive into prayer. Let's clean the slate before discussing prayer and the supernatural power it yields. I have prayed for you. Here is one you can pray over yourself as we begin. May you be blessed by his tender words of the soul. Thank you, Chet!

> *Holy Father, you alone are worthy of my praise and adoration. I am not worthy to come before you in the filth of my flesh. Thank you for imparting the righteousness of your Son upon me that I may approach your holy throne with confidence. Otherwise,*

I know I could not stand in the glory of your presence.

This day, I humble myself before you, understanding though I still sin and fall short of your glory, I am covered by the blood of Jesus and adopted as your son/daughter. I have done nothing to deserve your adoption. I can do nothing to deserve it. Only by your wonderful grace and mercy am I not consumed by my sin nor reserved for the curse sin has brought upon humanity. My most righteous works are nothing more than filthy rags in comparison to your holiness. Through your grace, I have been made whole. Father, please help me believe your truth in the deepest recesses of my heart so my feeling of unworthiness does not prevent me from boldly pursuing your will in my life.

Father, my flesh is weak. My flesh seeks to fulfill its desires. I know those desires bring about bondage. Thank you, for no longer am I a slave to sin. Please help me, Father, to live in the reality of such freedom. I often function as though sin is still my master, and I do not want to do that any longer. Father, please strengthen me in a way that only you can. Please protect me from the darts of the enemy. Help me to be keenly aware of when he flashes his lure before my eyes. Help me to see beyond the glimmering streak that promises to satisfy my appetite and to recognize that lurking beneath that enticing appeal is a set of hooks that will sink into my flesh and drag me in a direction that I do not want to go.

Father, please open my eyes and give me heavenly sight to see the lure for what it truly is: an appeal to my flesh to believe this world has more to offer me than you do. Father, please help me to reject the lie that you are keeping things from me that will make me happy and fulfill my needs.

By the power of your Holy Spirit, please plant your flag of truth deep within my soul—the truth that my deepest need is a relationship with my creator, and only that relationship can provide true fulfillment. Help me to be aware and to remember that following my flesh has always taken peace away from me. It has made me feel dirty. It has made me feel anxious. It has left me feeling naked and exposed. It has made me hide from you. It has made me conceal my deeds in darkness and avoid the light for fear of my wickedness being exposed. It has made me deceitful. It has made me a liar. It has prevented me from fulfilling my calling. It has been a barrier in my relationships with those I love. It has robbed me of the strength and ability to accomplish what you have set before me. It has caused pain for those I am re-

sponsible for protecting.

Father, please help me remember the lure is a false promise to satisfy my hunger. It always takes me to a place I do not want to be, with a hunger that has not been satisfied, a pain that has pierced my soul, and a hook firmly planted in me that continues to drag me away.

Father, I repent for my weakness and for continuing to take the bait even though I know better. Please forgive me for so often failing to be led by the Spirit. Please strengthen my faith in you as the Good Father. I have spent my inheritance on riotous living, wallowed in the mire, and eaten with the pigs.

Father, I return to you begging for your forgiveness. I see you running out to meet me with a ring and a cloak reserved only for your children. I feel the warmth and safety of your embrace. I ask you, Father, please renew me and make me whole. Please cut away any hooks that are left in me and hold me firmly in your net of safety. Please help me to delight in the righteousness of the kingdom and feast at your table. Please fill me so completely with your Spirit that there is no room to hunger for the things of this world. Please shield my eyes from the lures the enemy flashes before me. Please protect me from the trappings of his plans. Please help me stand boldly in the face of temptation and proclaim that I am a child of the King. Please help me walk in the light and have peace, knowing there is no darkness left within me to be exposed.

Father, I thank you for your merciful kindness. I thank you that I can call you Father.

In the power of the name of your son, Jesus Christ, I pray this prayer and receive your healing. Amen!

5

WE, AS FOLLOWERS OF THE WAY, ARE INSTRUCTED TO PRAY

I explained in the prior pages why prayer is essential to me, but what does the Bible say about prayer for us as followers of the Way (see John 14:6)? Here are a few scriptures encouraging us to a life of prayer. If we want to be completely accurate, the Bible does not just *encourage* us to pray. As you will see below in our first Bible reference, we are "exhorted" to pray. To exhort means to "strongly encourage or urge someone to do something; have a sense of pushing forward."(1) This passage's use of such a strong word suggests that God is trying to persuade us to pray.

> ... I urge that supplications, prayers, intercessions, and thanksgivings be made for all people, for kings and all who are in high positions, that we may lead a peaceful and quiet life, godly and dignified in every way. This is good, and it is pleasing in the sight of God our Savior.
>
> 1 Timothy 2:1-3

... Pray for us, that the word of the Lord may speed ahead and be honored, as happened among you, and that we may be delivered from wicked and evil men. For not all have faith. But the Lord is faithful. He will establish you and guard you against the evil one.
2 Thessalonians 3:1-3

Seek the welfare of the city I have deported you to. Pray to the LORD on its behalf, for when it has prosperity, you will prosper.
Jeremiah 29:7, HCSB

If my people, who are called by name, will humble themselves and pray and seek my face and turn from their wicked ways, then I will hear from heaven, and I will forgive their sin and will heal their land.
2 Chronicles 7:14

As you read the verses above, you see much instruction is given on prayer within. We see types of prayers, who to pray for, and why. I do not know about you, but the topic of prayer has never been one I have heard from the pulpit, and it was never a topical study for me until prayer became my life preserver. Are you excited to learn more? Me too. Let's keep going.

Jesus said to them, "I am the way, and the truth, and the life. No one comes to the Father except through me."
John 14:6

6

LORD, TEACH US TO PRAY

I accepted Christ as my Savior as a young child. However, I did not receive him as lord of my life until I was much older. When I first began an intimate spiritual journey in 2013, prayer catapulted me into a world of great excitement and joy as well as a world of unknowns. I would read prayers, watch people pray online, and get in front of as many praying people as possible.

I knew prayer had power. It was like refreshing waters on a hot, sun-parched day. I could feel the electricity of prayers the more and more I sat amid them. The atmosphere was charged, and so was I. Just as the disciples seemed to come to understand prayer was important during their time with Jesus and wanted to learn more, I, too, wanted to learn more.

The one noted request in the Word from the disciples to Jesus was, "Lord, teach us to pray" (Luke 11:1). If after all they saw, heard, and experienced, they thought it was a vital lesson to be learned, then it must be critical for you and me as believers as well.

One of my favorite quotes is from a praying warrior, Callie Shipp Gray, whom I listen to weekly on Facebook. Her testimony is, "My prayer life was caught, not taught."

What did she mean by that? She meant that no one sat her down and taught her how to pray and the vocabulary to pray, but in positioning herself in front of prayer warriors, she learned how to be a praying warrior. She recently recounted to her viewers that those moments sparked a fire within her as she witnessed and experienced the impact of those prayers prayed in her life and in those around her.

In his response to the disciple's question, Jesus gave a prayer example in Matthew 6:9-13 which we will read in chapter nine. His example serves as a foundation, a blueprint that could be replicated. We call that blueprint "The Lord's Prayer." It is an excellent model for how we should pray.

However, I believe that following Jesus for three years and witnessing the importance of prayer in his life and its impact on him and others probably left a much deeper impression on the disciples than one model prayer. In what appears to be a matter of seconds, Jesus gave the disciples a textbook lesson on prayer, but the internship lasted three years. I would be inclined to believe the disciples would "amen" Callie's testimony that prayer was more caught than taught.

> ... Jesus was praying in a certain place,
> and when he finished, one of his disciples said to him,
> "Lord, teach us to pray, as John taught his disciples."
> *Luke 11:1*

7

Avenues of Prayer

As we read earlier, 1 Timothy 2:1-3 says a well-woven prayer life includes *thanksgiving, praise, confession,* and *supplication*. Below, you will find a few sample verses. What you will read below is not an exhaustive list, but it will drive home the idea I am trying to convey. May these verses boost your awareness of the different avenues of prayer and provide further examples of just how diverse one's prayer life can be.

When our daughters were young, I drew a picture of a heart with four chambers and taped it to their bathroom mirrors. Within each of the four chambers, I listed either thanksgiving, praise, confession, or supplication. I did this to remind our daughters that as they go through their day and pray, they should not just petition Heaven for all their desires but also season their prayers with these other ingredients.

Thanksgiving: The expression of gratitude, especially to God. (2)

Praise: The expression of approval or admiration of

someone or something. (3)

Confession: A formal statement admitting one is guilty of a crime. (4)

Supplication: The act of asking or begging for something earnestly or humbly. (5)

You might be asking, "Where are examples of these avenues of prayer in the Bible?" I am glad you asked. Here are just a few:

> Pray without ceasing, ***give thanks*** in all circumstances; for this is the will of God in Christ Jesus for you.
> *1 Thessalonians 5:17-18*

> In the days of his flesh, Jesus offered up prayers and ***supplications***, with loud cries and tears, to him who was able to save him from death, and he was heard because of his reverence.
> *Hebrews 5:7*

> The one who conceals his sins will not prosper, but whoever ***confesses*** and renounces them will find mercy.
> *Proverbs 28:13, HCSB*

> I will bless the Lord at all times; his ***praise*** shall continually be in my mouth.
> *Psalm 34:1*

Want to explore more? I have made it easy by providing a few more scriptures below. I recommend doing a word search in a concordance for each of the four avenues to see what other verses you find. A concordance has become one of my favorite study tools.

Ephesians 6:18   1 Timothy 2:1   Leviticus 5:5
Psalm 100:4, 150:6   1 John 1:9

If I were you, I would be asking myself, *What does it look like when I utilize these avenues of prayer in my own prayer life?*

Below are a few sample prayers I have written using each of the four avenues of prayer.

> *Father God, as I wake and before my feet hit the floor to start my day, I want to **thank you** for keeping me and my family safe through the night and allowing me to see another day. Please guide me so my day begins and ends as a sweet aroma to you. In Jesus's name, amen!*

> *Father God, I **praise** your holy name. May the breath of my mouth always **praise** you. I **praise** you in the morning, I **praise** you at noon, and I **praise** you as the sun goes down. I **praise** you when I am happy and when I am sad. I will **praise** you forever, for in your salvation, I am always glad.*

> *Father God, I **confess** the frustration and doubt within my heart. While I have seen your wonders and experienced your healing too many times to recall, I am struggling to trust you with the unknown of my current ailments and your timeline for resolution. Father, while I do believe, please help me overcome my unbelief. In Jesus's name, amen!*

> *Father God, I am witnessing so many people around the country lifting **supplication** to you. Please hear their cries and collect their tears. May the **supplication** of the multitudes move your heart in our great nation to deliver us from the hands of the wicked. May our nation be a beacon of light to the entire world, illuminating peace, joy, unity, and love to all. May every tear you gather water the soil of our nation, not just for the here and now but for the generations to come. In Jesus's name, amen!*

Now, it's time to write a few of your own. Here's a challenge for you: Set a timer for five or ten minutes, pick one avenue of prayer, and write as many prayers as possible with that one word. Invite friends and family to the challenge. Share your prayers with others on your social media with the hashtag #prayerispowerful.

Was the challenge easy? Hard? Awkward?

I wish someone had walked me through this at an early age. In many churches, teaching personal prayer rarely advances from milk to meat. As a result, far too many people remain juveniles and never progress beyond reciting childhood prayers such as, "Thank you, Jesus, for this food" or "Now I lay me down to sleep." I hate to admit it, but I continued blabbering those rehearsed prayers long after getting married and having children. I was well on my way to passing on that generational blabbering to our girls as well.

Don't get me wrong—there is nothing wrong with those prayers and even teaching those to your children. Everyone must start somewhere. However, like infants, the goal is to grow. Therefore, our prayer life should mature with time as well.

I have come to understand that prayer is far more profound, powerful, and communicative than rote prayers. No relationship would have depth or longevity with only recited scripts to speak to one another. The conversations with our Heavenly Father, Lord, and Savior are no different.

Later, you will be invited to take your "prayer temperature" to gauge how cold or hot your prayer life is. Wherever you find yourself in this moment, no matter how cold or hot, do not fret or beat yourself up. No shame here! My prayer for you is that the flame of your prayer life will grow with each prayer into a roaring fire that spreads to all you encounter each day and leaves a legacy of ignited prayers throughout the generations to come. The only lousy prayer is the one that remains in one's heart—never uttered and never lifted to the Father.

> First of all, then, I urge that supplications, prayers, intercessions, and thanksgivings be made for all people, for kings and all who are in high positions, that we may lead a peaceful and quiet life, godly and dignified in every way. This is good, and it is pleasing in the sight of God our Savior...
> *1 Timothy 2:1-3*

8

Prayer Examples in the Bible

Our prayers fill in the gaps between Heaven and Earth. Gaps are the darkness wherein the enemy lies in wait. When we pray, we unite with all of Heaven to commission the hand of the Father to move on our behalf and the behalf of others. Our prayers create bridges and lifelines to the ear of the Father when others do not know how to pray or even if they need to.

Several years ago, I dreamed of standing on the threshold of my paternal grandparents' home. There was a gap between the inside and the outside. I had one foot on each side. I woke, and the Lord gave me the understanding that I was the bridge for that side of my family line. I was bridging the gap between my family and his throne through my prayers. He spoke to my spirit and said, *With each generation, I await someone who will stand in the gap for the family line.*

That message from the Lord had a two-fold effect on me. It was exciting and hopeful to hear that my prayers were making a difference and Heaven had taken notice. But it also grieved me that right now, all over the earth, there are families out there with no one standing in the gap for theirs. Each family, each community, each ... You get the idea. Each _____ (fill in the blank) needs our prayers. Just think of how many people are standing next to you in line at the grocery store or how many people you drive by every day on the roads that have no one praying for them. Praying for their salvation, deliverance, or peace. The Bible has so many examples of prayers prayed and answered. May each of us grab hold of this message and pray, pray, pray.

Throughout the Bible, numerous prayers and praises are lifted to the Father. Once I began reading through the Bible each year, I started noticing just how many prayers I could highlight and recite over myself, my family, and others. As you pick up your Bible, I highly suggest that you start noting each time you read a prayer. I place a "P" with a circle around it next to each prayer I find as a marker and reminder. I have heard of others highlighting each prayer in a specific color. Just have fun with it. Be creative! I will often put my name or the names of my family members in the prayers from the Bible and print them out so that I can use them when petitioning the Father on their behalf during my prayer time. This makes the prayers personal and brings the Word to life for me.

When we personalize the prayers of the Bible, we can continue to make the Bible relevant to our everyday experiences and not just to those in distant history. While I also love the letters and stories the scribes of the Bible have brought forth, it is their prayers that connect me to the hearts of our brothers and sisters of a time gone by. The Word is alive and able to resuscitate the coldest souls—no matter the day or hour.

On the next page, you will find a few prayer examples from the Bible that I felt led to share. These prayers model how we can pray and how our prayers affect the world, and they also highlight key moments of prayer in the Scripture.

Our prayers move the hand of the Father to commission

angels on our behalf.

> ... your words have been heard, and I have come because of your words.
>
> *Daniel 10:12*

Our prayers can deliver a people group—even an entire nation—from annihilation.

> ... Behold, I have given Esther the house of Haman, and they have hanged him on the gallows, because he intended to lay hands on the Jews.
>
> *Esther 8:7*

When was the first time we see the people of the Bible begin to call upon the Lord?

> ... At that time people began to call upon the name of the Lord.
>
> *Genesis 4:26*

What is the last prayer of the Bible?

> ... Come, Lord Jesus! The grace of the Lord Jesus be with all. Amen.
>
> *Revelation 22:20-21*

What are five well-known, powerful prayers lifted to the Father by a few people in the Bible?

The next few verses were the top web search results for "prayers in the Bible." These prayers were powerful enough to move the hand of the Father in the days of old, and that same Father and power are alive and well for you today. Be bold! Pick up the phone of faith and call upon the Lord today. Adapt them and pray them over your family for the next thirty days.

> The Lord bless you and keep you; the Lord make his face to shine upon you and be gracious to you; the Lord lift up his countenance upon you and give you peace.
> *Numbers 6:24-26*

> Jabez called upon the God of Israel, saying, "Oh that you would bless me and enlarge my border, and that your hand might be with me, and that you would keep me from harm so that it might not bring me pain!" And God granted what he asked.
> *1 Chronicles 4:10*

> ... It is my prayer that your love may abound more and more, with knowledge and all discernment, so that you may approve what is excellent, and so be pure and blameless for the day of Christ, filled with the fruit of righteousness that comes through Jesus Christ, to the glory and praise of God.
> *Philippians 1:9-11*

> May the God of hope fill you with all joy and peace in believing, so that by the power of the Holy Spirit you may abound in hope.
> *Romans 15:13*

> Remove far from me falsehood and lying;
> give me neither poverty nor riches;
> feed me with the food that is needful for me,
> lest I be full and deny you and say,
> "Who is the Lord?" or lest I be poor and steal

and profane the name of my God.
Proverbs 30:8-9

For a deeper study, I've included a few more verses for you to look up and pray for yourself and others.

Psalm 37:1-9; 51; 70:4	Philippians 1:9-11
Luke 23:34	Colossians 1:9-14
Ephesians 1:15-23; 3:14-21	John 17:1-4
Lamentations 3:22-26	Jonah 2:1-9

In the next chapter, I'll share with you my top three favorite prayers from the Bible, which I have adapted and pray for myself and my family often.

9

My Foundational Prayers

You will find three of what I believe to be the most powerful prayers of the Word, which I recite often: Lord's Prayer, Psalm 91, and lastly, the Armor Prayer. I say these out loud and declare them for myself and my family regularly. Pray these prayers with me, adding your name and the names of those for whom you are interceding.

I clung to these when I was going through some of the worst storms of life. There were days I would repeat them endlessly. Reciting and reflecting on the words and truths of these prayers brought me so much comfort and peace when nothing else seemed to work. I highly recommend you print these out for you and your family and save them in the notes app on your phone. When the storms of life begin to roll in, you can refer to these and allow them to strengthen you until the storm passes and the rays of the sun break through. For behind every cloud, the sun always shines. We need shelter to run to until it does. Prayer places us in the Father's presence—the fortress of protection amid any storm.

Lord's Prayer
Matthew 6:9-13, HCSB

Our Father in heaven,
your name be honored as holy.
Your kingdom come.
Your will be done
on earth as it is in heaven.
Give us today our daily bread.
And forgive us our debts,
as we also have forgiven our debtors.
And do not bring us into temptation
but deliver us from the evil one.
For yours is the kingdom and
the power and the glory forever.
Amen.

My Refuge and My Fortress
Psalm 91

He who dwells in the shelter of the Most High
will abide in the shadow of the Almighty.
I will say to the Lord, "My refuge and my fortress,
my God, in whom I trust."
For he will deliver you from the snare of the fowler
and from the deadly pestilence.
He will cover you with his pinions,
and under his wings you will find refuge;
his faithfulness is a shield and buckler.
You will not fear the terror of the night,
nor the arrow that flies by day,
nor the pestilence that stalks in darkness,
nor the destruction that wastes at noonday.
A thousand may fall at your side,
ten thousand at your right hand,

but it will not come near you.
You will only look with your eyes
and see the recompense of the wicked.
Because you have made the Lord
your dwelling place the Most High,
who is my refuge no evil shall be allowed to befall you,
no plague come near your tent.
For he will command his angels
concerning you to guard you in all your ways.
On their hands they will bear you up,
lest you strike your foot against a stone.
You will tread on the lion and the adder;
the young lion and the serpent
you will trample underfoot.
"Because he holds fast to me in love, I will deliver him;
I will protect him, because he knows my name.
When he calls to me, I will answer him;
I will be with him in trouble;
I will rescue him and honor him.
With long life I will satisfy him
and show him my salvation."

The Whole Armor of God
Ephesians 6:10-20

Finally, be strong in the Lord
and in the strength of his might.
Put on the whole armor of God
that you may be able to stand
against the schemes of the devil,
for we do not wrestle against flesh and blood,
but against the rulers, against the authorities,
against the cosmic powers over this present darkness
and against the spiritual forces of evil in the heavenly places.
Therefore, take up the whole armor of God,
that you may be able to withstand in the evil day,

and having done all, to stand firm.
Stand therefore, having fastened on the belt of truth,
and having put on the breastplate of righteousness,
and, as shoes for your feet, having put on the readiness
given by the gospel of peace.
In all circumstances take up the shield of faith,
with which you can extinguish
all the flaming darts of the evil one;
and take the helmet of salvation,
and the sword of the Spirit,
which is the word of God,
praying at all times in the Spirit,
with all prayer and supplication.
To that end, keep alert with all perseverance,
making supplication for all the saints,
and for myself, that words may be given to me
in opening my mouth boldly to proclaim
the mystery of the gospel,
for which I am an ambassador in chains,
that I may declare it boldly,
as I ought to speak.

As I began to learn about the armor of God years ago, I printed out an image like the one on the next page and taped it to every mirror in every bathroom of our home. I love visuals! I wanted to be sure that each of us had a visual reminder to pray daily, putting on the whole armor of God.

Armor of God

"Therefore take up the whole armor of God, that you may be able to withstand the evil day, and having done all, to stand firm."
Ephesians 6:13

(6)

Our physical attire is essential. However, our spiritual armor is *vital*! Just like a police officer putting on armor before work in the morning, as warriors of Christ, we should clothe ourselves in spiritual armor before we begin our day. Officers arm themselves *before* they hit the streets because they know there is real danger waiting for them. We, too, need to suit up every morning in prayer and worship to arm ourselves for the day ahead.

We should not wait to clothe ourselves in the spiritual armor of God until the end of the day. Waiting until work is done for the day leaves us exhausted, weary, and unable to give the Lord our best. When we bring our firstfruits to the Lord every morning, we honor him by giving him the first minutes of our day.

The visual below is of a police officer and their gear. Visuals are great teaching aids and quick-glance reminder tools. In the Bible, Paul uses the imagery of a soldier prepared for battle to illustrate how we are to prepare for the spiritual battles we encounter daily. Today, the image of a police officer's gear may be much more relatable.

Similar to the armor of God, each item of a police officer's gear serves a purpose to help protect them and enable them to accomplish their duties. You can think of their bulletproof vests as shields of faith. Kevlar helmets as helmets of salvation. You get the idea. They must have their gear on them as their shift begins.

(7)

I kept these printouts in my prayer nook as a constant reminder of the battle being waged 24/7 against our souls. We must be armed and ready! It also reminded me that I have a part to play in my readiness for battle by suiting up in God's Word and standing firm in him to do the rest. I give God my best, and he takes care of the rest!

As we submit our days to him, it communicates to God that we understand that he is our provider and protector, and our lives are entrusted to him. It takes me back to the Psalm 91 prayer, which states, "God is our shelter and fortress." I think of his shelter and fortress as our spiritual Iron Dome Defense System.

"The Iron Dome Defense System is the Israeli military's missile defense system to protect against incoming short-range weapons. It operates in all weather conditions and uses radar to track rockets. It can differentiate between those that are likely to hit built-up areas and those that are not." (8) I envision the devil's attacks as incoming missiles, and prayerfully, I can rest assured that God is protecting me so long as I remain in his Iron Dome of protection. When I pray for the protection of myself and my family, I often ask the Father to place us within his Iron Dome Defense System.

Prayer is our most special conversation of the day and our greatest weapon of warfare. It is a time for you to share your cares and concerns with the Father and for him to speak directly to your soul. Who is better to speak to us concerning all matters of life than the one who created it all, our Heavenly Father?

Above, I provided real-life examples of things we can do to "suit up" and prepare ourselves, as we are told in Ephesians, to be ready and armed for daily spiritual battles. In pondering that thought, I was reminded of the Bible story in Nehemiah 3 when the Israelites were commissioned to rebuild the wall that would surround and protect Jerusalem. The Word says the men grabbed a tool to work in one hand and a weapon in the other to be ready for any attacks while they were actively building.

Wow! I cannot imagine working under those circumstances, but they did what was necessary to accomplish God's plan.

It is time for each of us to be more alert and proactive about the daily spiritual battle against us and our families. The Word says in 1 Peter 5:8, "Be sober-minded; be watchful. Your adversary, the devil, prowls around like a roaring lion, seeking someone to devour."

Let that sink in! As a spiritual being, the devil never sleeps or goes on holiday. He and his minions are forever, at all times, looking to devour us. Is the prowling devil something to fear? No! 2 Timothy 1:7 says, "For God gave us a spirit not of fear but of power and love and self-control," and James 4:7 tells us, "Submit yourselves therefore to God. Resist the devil, and he will flee from you." So, while we should not be fearful, it is something we should be mindful of daily.

We are forever in a spiritual war against a spiritual army seeking to penetrate every area of our lives, not for our good but for our ultimate demise. Darkness has nothing to offer, for there is no life found within it, but the enemies of God's light are consistently trying to lure us into that darkness with empty promises and pleasures.

I have found many Christians leave praying and intercession to the church's leaders and the patriarchs of families. To have just anyone pray, especially women and children, was somewhat foreign to me. The Christians who did pray typically reserved it for the dinner table, bedtime, and the bedsides of the sick and dying, and I did the same for a long time. Now, after reading the Bible for myself, I have come to know and understand that prayer is for everyone. 'Everyone' is all people of all time. I have previously pointed out several scriptures that provide biblical evidence of this truth. Remember, we are all instructed to pray and "pray without ceasing."

One of the main reasons God wants us to pray and be armed and ready is to keep the identity of our true enemy in the forefront of our minds. Neither God, nor our spouses, neighbors, bosses, professors, etc., are our enemy—Satan is. As the Word states in Ephesians 6:12, our true enemies are "the rulers, authorities, cosmic powers over this present darkness, spiritual forces of evil in the heavenly places."

Armed with a mindset of truth, we begin to see and understand the world and other humans through a different lens. We come to offer grace and mercy once we understand our true adversary is Satan—who is at work commissioning every poke and prod—rather than the individuals we encounter in our everyday lives. They are the weapon rather than the warring enemy.

These spiritual beings spend their entire existence trying to manipulate, divide, destroy, and agitate all of us into fighting one another. Thus, we will be distracted and angry with one another rather than picking up our tools to expand the kingdom of God here on earth. We need to be picking up weapons to wage war against the enemy's tactics instead of against one another.

May we all grab a tool and get to work! And do not forget to grab a weapon of prayer with the other hand. You never know who along your journey may benefit from your thoughtful pause of prayer.

For we do not wrestle against flesh and blood, but against the rulers, against the authorities, against the cosmic powers over this present darkness, against the spiritual forces of evil in the heavenly places.
Ephesians 6:12

... One of the elders said to me, "Weep no more; behold, the Lion of the tribe of Judah, the Root of David, has conquered..."
Revelation 5:5

10

JESUS AND PRAYER

> And rising very early **in the morning**, while it was still dark, he departed and went out to a desolate place, and there he prayed.
> *Mark 1:35*

We have looked at the most common prayers of the Bible. We have explored my favorite prayers. We have even read a few prayer samples, which the Bible's writers offered up in years gone by. If we wrote down each and noted them here, we would see that prayer permeates the pages of the Word. And yet, what stands out the most to me in all of it is Jesus's devotion to prayer.

Jesus, our example, often separated himself from the noise and the crowds to sit before his Father in prayer. Maybe you caught that the verse above reads, "... in the morning." Jesus, like a police officer, understands the battle and knows that to enter the wars along the paths we will travel, we must put on our "spiritual" armor and tool belt in the morning. As Christians, our weapons of warfare are prayer and the Word.

Let's look at what Scripture says about Jesus's prayer life.

Did Jesus's life model one of prayer for us?

What can we glean from the recordings of Jesus's prayer life?

Jesus often went away from the crowds to be alone before the Father and sometimes took the whole night to pray. Yep, the whole night. Have you ever been so burdened you spent an entire night alone in prayer?

> After He had sent the crowds away, He **went up on the mountain by Himself to pray**; and when it was evening, He was there alone.
> *Matthew 14:23*

> But **he would withdraw** to **desolate places** and **pray**.
> *Luke 5:16*

> In these days he **went out to the mountain to pray**, and **all night he continued in prayer** to God.
> *Luke 6:12*

Jesus often prayed with great emotion and fervor.

> In the days of his flesh, Jesus offered up prayers and **supplications**, with loud cries and tears, to him who was able to save him from death, and he was heard because of his reverence. (9)
> *Hebrews 5:7*

> And going a little farther, **he fell on the ground and prayed** that, if it were possible, the hour might pass from him.
> *Mark 14:35*

Jesus intercedes for us and is our example of how to intercede for others.

> Therefore, He is always able to save those who come to God through Him, since *He always lives to intercede for them.*
> *Hebrews 7:25, HCSB*

> Who is to condemn? *Christ Jesus* is the one who died—more than that, who was raised—who is at the right hand of God, who indeed *is interceding for us*.
> *Romans 8:34*

> ... he bore the sin of many, and *makes intercession* for the transgressors.
> *Isaiah 53:12*

> ... *I have prayed for you* that your faith may not fail. And when you have turned again, strengthen your brothers.
> *Luke 22:32*

What does intercession mean?

Intercession: the act of interceding, prayer, petition, or entreaty in favor of another. (10)

One of the most beautiful and humble acts of honor to the Father is to intercede in prayer on behalf of others. Those acts are most fervently expressed when intercessory prayers are prayed for total strangers. What greater act of sacrifice and love for humanity outside of laying down one's own life can one offer other than to call upon the mighty hand of the Father to move on a stranger's behalf? This is a selfless act because they will likely never know on this side of Heaven what you have done.

Jesus's love and sacrifice were expressed through his prayers for us while on earth, but they did not cease with his ascension to Heaven. Remember Hebrews 7:25 from earlier? Jesus continues interceding for us even from his seat next to the Heavenly Father. His example expresses the great value the Father places on intercessory prayer. We, as his children, should take this example to heart.

What would a personal example of intercessory prayer look like today?

I can remember hearing a story several years ago about a person in our community who was a member of a local church and had been struggling to release their addiction to smoking to the Lord. When I heard that, I felt led to add their name to my prayer list, which I kept in my shower.

"Why the shower?" you might ask. Because, in the shower, one is in an isolated location with nothing else to do with their brain power, so we might as well use that time to intercede for others.

After several years of praying for this individual (unbeknownst to them), I heard that they had been completely delivered from their addiction to smoking. Praise Jesus! Am I so prideful to think my prayers were the only reason this person was set free from their addiction? No! However, I bet my prayers didn't hurt. Maybe one day, the Lord will show me a slide-show in Heaven of how my prayers were woven into the tapestry of their freedom testimony.

Earlier, I mentioned reciting prayers and rote prayers. I do not know about you, but I have had times when I felt shame and guilt for praying the same prayer multiple times. I would beat myself up and tell myself I must not have enough faith, or I would only pray once about something and trust it was resolved whether I saw the answer yet or not. I am so grateful Jesus shows us through his prayer life that it is perfectly reasonable to petition the Father in prayer multiple times for the same need.

Jesus was persistent in prayer, often bringing the same heart cry before the Father.

> ***Again, for the second time***, he ***went away and prayed***, "My Father, if this cannot pass unless I drink it, your will be done."
> *Matthew 26:42*

> *... **Leaving them again**, he **went away and prayed** for the **third time**, saying the same words again.*
> *Matthew 26:44*

> ***Again, He went away and prayed, saying the same words.***
> *Mark 14:39*

And, if that is not enough, when I feel shame trying to cast its shadow over me, the Holy Spirit reminds me of the parable in the Bible about the "persistent widow." Do you know the story? If not, commit it to memory so the next time the enemy starts whispering condemnation and shame, you can remind him of the Word and God's heart for the persistence of prayer.

The Parable of the Persistent Widow
Luke 18:1-8

And he told them a parable to the effect that they ought always to pray and not lose heart. He said, "In a certain city there was a judge who neither feared God nor respected man. And there was a widow in that city who kept coming to him and saying, 'Give me justice against my adversary.' For a while he refused, but afterward, he said to himself, 'Though I neither fear God nor respect man, yet because this widow keeps bothering me, I will give her justice so that she will not beat me down by her continual coming.'" And the Lord said, "Hear what the unrighteous judge says. And will not God give justice to his elect, who cry to him day and night? Will he delay long over them? I tell you; he will give justice to them speedily. Nevertheless, when the Son of Man comes, will he find faith on earth?"

11

The Words of Your Mouth Declare Your Destiny

What does your mouth and declaring your destiny have to do with prayer? Think of it as a secret weapon in our prayer arsenal. I consider it the stealth bomber of prayer.

Many years ago, I was standing outside in our backyard when an enormous shadow was suddenly cast on the ground around me. Startled, I looked up to see a massive, black, unidentified flying object that appeared to be hovering over our home. I never heard it approach, and I never heard it cross over. There was no sound at all as it glided away.

And it was so close! I had never seen a plane fly that close to the ground. It was completely unlike any aircraft I had ever seen. Let me say upfront: I do not believe in aliens. However, I had no reference to any such flying craft. At that moment, it was a UFO to me.

I quickly called my husband at work and told him what I had just witnessed. As I was talking to him, he was standing outside on the golf course where he worked, and he saw the same aircraft flying over his head.

"That's a stealth bomber," he said. "It's probably headed down to the air force base below us."

Just like that stealth bomber, using the words of your mouth as a weapon is powerful and often sneaks up on the enemy when he least expects it from us.

Where am I going with this train of thought? What am I talking about? I am talking about talking! Starting in Genesis 1:3 and continuing throughout the chapter, we read the account of God himself "speaking" everything into existence. It was through his voice, his utterances, and his breath that all we see and know was created. Psalm 33:9, states, "For he spoke, and it came to be; he commanded, and it stood firm." We also read in Job 22:28, 1599 Geneva Bible, "Thou shalt also decree a thing, and he shall establish it unto thee, and the light shall shine upon thy ways." Like our Heavenly Father, there is power in our utterances.

Have I ever heard of or known anyone to speak a tree or a house into existence before my eyes? No! However, God does tell us life and death are held within our mouths. Therefore, we must be careful what proceeds from our lips.

How can we harness the power of our tongues for kingdom good? We can utilize this weapon—the weapon of our words—to *speak* forth our prayers and declare and establish what we want to see in our lives and the lives of others.

Here is an example of a prayer I might speak out loud regularly until I see salvation manifest in a family member's life:

> *Father God, I come before you and declare the Lord's salvation over my nephew. I declare life and not death over him and ask you to commission your angels to minister to his soul and surround him with your sheep to raise him in truth and love. In Jesus's name, amen!*

We must also be mindful of speaking words that bring life, not death. Proverbs 18:21 states, "Death and life are in the power of the tongue, and those who love it will eat its fruits." And, in Proverbs 6:2, HCSB, we are warned we can be "trapped by the words of our lips and ensnared by the words of our mouth."

Furthermore, we see in James 4:2-3, HCSB, "... You do not have because you do not ask. You ask and don't receive because you ask with wrong motives, so that you may spend it on your evil desires." For our prayers to be answered, we must pray per God's will and not our limited, self-serving desires.

Here's an example of a prayer one would not want to pray:

> *Father God, please remove Tilly from her position at the bank and give the job to Marsha. I like Marsha more; she is much nicer. Thank you! In Jesus's name, amen!*

That prayer is motivated by one's flesh and not likely according to God's will. We must be mindful of the words we speak. Mathew 12:36-37 states, "I tell you, on the day of judgment people will give account for every careless word they speak, for by your words you will be justified, and by your words, you will be condemned."

Here's another example of a prayer one would not want to pray:

> *Father God, I declare my son, James, will be a doctor when he grows up. In Jesus's name, amen!*

You might say, "But I want my son to be a doctor. Every man in our family has been a doctor for the last hundred years. Why not pray a prayer like that?" We would not do so because God tells us to pray according to his will. James is only two months old. Only God knows if he will be a doctor or even the President of the United States. What type of prayer might one pray instead?

> *Father God, thank you for James. If it is your will for James to be a doctor like the other men in our family when he grows up, please help us raise him so that he will be the most loving, honest, and effective doctor in his field. If that is not your will, Father, please prepare our hearts for the path you have for him so that we ultimately raise him to walk in love and truth and follow your will for his life. In Jesus's name, amen!*

When we speak our prayers out loud, they carry power and a frequency that sends a chill down the enemy's spine. When I wake up each morning, I want the enemy's team to say, "Oh no! She's awake!" I want his army to know I am a fierce, unstoppable, prayer-warring momma. I want them to regret even thinking of coming against me and my household.

By that same token, I do not want to speak forth utterances from my mouth that the enemy will take and use as weapons of warfare against myself or others.

Father God, may the words of my mouth and the meditation of my heart be acceptable in your sight, O Lord, my rock, and my redeemer. In Jesus's name, amen!

> Let the words of my mouth, and the meditation of my heart
> be acceptable in your sight, O Lord, my rock and my redeemer.
> *Psalm 19:14*

12

Why am I not Seeing My Prayers Answered?

Okay. Stop for a second, hold your hand up before your mouth, and breathe out. Did you feel your breath hit your hand? Then guess what? You are alive! There is not a soul alive, or passed-on for that matter, that has ever prayed that has not, in their minds, had prayers go "unanswered." Let's take a look at what the Bible has to say about why your prayers may not be answered.

One has not because they ask not—James 4:2

This one is simple. We can go along in life without resolving our heart's desires, questions, and longings simply because we are not praying and seeking answers and wisdom from the Father.

One has not because they do not ask according to the will of the Father—1 John 5:14

This was a huge 'ouch' when I read it. What a time of self-reflection, huh? Could many of our prayers be going unanswered because we are not seeking the will of the

Father for our lives and his kingdom purposes but for our fleshly desires? It sounds like it.

One has not because they ask the Father with wrong motives—James 4:3

Yikes! Again, 'ouch'! That one hurt a bit, too. It makes me want to pause and check my heart and motives before I allow prayer to flow. Why am I praying this prayer? Who is to benefit? Would this prayer glorify my Father and advance his kingdom or my own?

I believe all prayers are answered and that not one returns void. Sometimes, our prayers are not answered in the way we wanted or expected, which makes them *seem* to go unanswered. Other times, we may never see the fruition of our prayers in this life.

For example, I once heard a testimony recounted online of a mother that had prayed forty years for her son to give his life to Christ, but she never saw this prayer answered. However, her son *did* give his life to Christ—at her funeral. That mother's prayers were answered, just not in her lifetime.

We have to have faith that our prayers will be answered according to God's perfect will and timeline.

13

Biblical Examples of Firstfruit Offerings

We have discussed types of prayer and the importance of prayer, but let's take that thought to an even deeper level of consideration. Have you ever considered there may be a time to pray that would be better than others throughout your day? Did you see the title of this chapter? Maybe the topic of firstfruits is new to you. It was for me until recently.

In the Bible, we see examples of firstfruit offerings by way of first-born children, grains, and animals. Although that looks much different now, the Old Testament clearly expresses that our Father in Heaven desires us to come before him with our best and with unrushed lives—not with our leftovers. These days, one's firstfruits might be giving God the firsts of our time, talents, and treasures. Just as your spouse or children would want your undivided attention, your Heavenly Father does too.

There are times in all our lives when we come before the Lord with our pain, sickness, burdens, and cares, which cannot and should not be the totality of our time spent before the Lord in communication and intimacy. If that were the case, no relationship would last, nor be healthy and desirable.

Giving God our firstfruits each morning arms us and sets the crooked places straight within our soul. It maps out our day to be God-focused and God-reliant, as well as allowing the Holy Spirit to fill us with the love of the Father so we can pour that love out for those we encounter throughout our day. I do not know about you, but I need that filling of love daily. No one wants Cristy without the Holy Spirit—that I can promise you! I need him to pour into me so that fresh, clean, living water pours out of me.

Suit up! Fill up! Arm yourself in prayer and go out there and pour into the dry wells of others you encounter as you go! Below, you will find biblical examples of firstfruits mentioned in the Word.

> We obligate ourselves to bring the firstfruits of our ground and the firstfruits of all fruit of every tree, year by year, to the house of the LORD; also to bring to the house of our God, to the priests who minister in the house of our God, the firstborn of our sons and of our cattle, as it is written in the Law, and the firstborn of our herds and of our flocks; and to bring the first of our dough, and our contributions, the fruit of every tree, the wine and the oil, to the priests, to the chambers of the house of our God; and to bring to the Levites the tithes from our ground, for it is the Levites who collect the tithes in all our towns where we labor.
> *Nehemiah 10:35-37*

> You shall take some of the first of all the fruit of the ground, which you harvest from your land that the LORD your God is giving you, and you shall put it in a basket, and you shall go to the place that the LORD your God will choose, to make his name to dwell there.
> *Deuteronomy 26:2*

> The best of the firstfruits of your ground you shall bring into the house of the Lord your God.
>
> *Exodus 23:19*

You can explore the topic of firstfruits more on your own. Here are some verses to expand your understanding:

Leviticus 23:9-14, 17-20   Deuteronomy 18:4; 26:10
Ezekiel 44:30   Numbers 15:20-21

Understanding the idea of firstfruits and the precedence the Bible places on it is important. We can also better understand Jesus's example (which we read about in previous pages) of getting up early, getting alone, and praying.

Although his time here on Earth was short, Jesus made a huge impact on every life he touched then, and that impact will continue for all of eternity. His prayers prayed then and those that continue from the right hand of the Father are shaping cultures and timelines from everlasting to everlasting. Never forget that your life, no matter how long or short, can impact the kingdom of God Almighty.

14

IN THE DAYS AHEAD

As we begin to wrap up our time together, let's discuss how we might apply what we have learned. You may be thinking, *This information is great, but what does implementing this information look like for me as I wake up tomorrow?*

1. **Firstfruits:** Start each day by dedicating the day to the Lord, remembering those firstfruits.
2. **Armor of God:** Put on your armor. We must be armed and ready for whatever life brings before we hit the streets each day, not just waiting to toss up 911 prayers should an event arise.
3. **Avenues of Prayer:** Remember you can always incorporate the four avenues of prayer—thanksgiving, praise, confession, and supplication—into your prayer time.
4. **Covering Prayer:** Pray a covering prayer over yourself, your family, your community... You get the idea. This prayer can be whatever the Lord leads you to. You may pray Psalm 91, or you may even be led to write your own. That is the beauty of prayer. It is just a sweet conversation with

your Father above. It does not have to be long or scripted. It just needs to be honest, open, and from the heart.

5. Prayer Journal: Start a prayer journal where you write down your prayers each day. You never know—the Lord may lead you to make those into a book one day.

6. Value of Prayer: The main point I hope you gather from this book is that prayer is valuable. It is worthwhile for you and your family, but it doesn't stop there. Your prayers can reach far beyond your physical presence and positioning. Prayer is a call to action for us as believers. Prayer is universal and timeless. Prayer is for speaking life not only into the present but also for the generations to come long after us.

7. Practice: Pray. Pray. Pray. Pray without ceasing!

15

THERE ARE NO ACCIDENTS IN THE KINGDOM OF GOD

Nothing in your life is insignificant. That has become abundantly clear to me over the past several years. After all, look what one invitation to church lead to.

As we wrap up this study on prayer, I thought I would revisit the beginning and expand a bit about my story so you can see the impact that one person or one moment can make in the life of another and for the kingdom of God. I have already shared that I am an "open your book of life and read it" kind of person. God drew me that way.

In an earlier chapter, I shared what events in my life led to my strong connection to and fervent belief in the power of prayer. What culminated in the writing of this book? Many people have powerful testimonies every day, but not all of them go out and start writing for the kingdom.

A sweet young lady befriended our youngest daughter at school shortly after our move to Tennessee ten years ago. She invited her to church one Sunday, and our whole family attended. That visit led us to make that church our home for a time. While attending that church, I met a lady, Ashley, and we became friends. Years later, after both of us had been called to fellowship with other groups of believers and disconnected, Ashley randomly tagged me in an online prayer group that prays together every weekday over Facebook Live. I watched that first day, and three years later, I am still watching and praying with that group every Monday through Friday.

While I was watching one day, the leader of the prayer group, Callie, had a few guests filling in for her and praying with us. Those women happened to live just outside of Nashville and had started a women's ministry that met monthly in the area. I looked up the ministry on Facebook and attended their next meeting. I attended the next several meetings, until life ultimately made me unavailable. During my time there, I had the opportunity to hear great speakers who spoke encouragement and the words I needed to hear in that season of life. It was a blessing!

Fast-forward about two years to when I recently completed what I thought would be my first and only book. I asked the Lord to lead me to what was next. Since the book was his calling, I trusted him to provide each step of the way. One night, as I began to pray before bed, I told God I needed help and asked who would lead me.

Then, as I slept that first night, I saw a woman's face several times in my dreams. Even as I woke, I saw her face. I knew immediately it was one of the women who spoke during one of the prayer gatherings I had attended in Nashville. However, I was not exactly sure which lady. I jumped out of bed and began searching Facebook to figure out who the woman was that God was showing me in the night. It did not take me long to find her. There she was! Lynn Eldridge, a published author to boot. I thought, *Okay, God, I found her. Now what?*

Instantly, I felt I was to reach out to her and tell her about my book and what God had shown me. My second thought was, *No way!* I sat on that thought with my stomach in knots all day. Once my husband returned home from work, I told him everything that had transpired. He simply said,

"Reach out to her."

I said, "No way. You're crazy, and she'll think I am crazy. 'Umm... Hey, God told me to reach out to you.' I am sure that will go over well."

But, I could not stop thinking about it. After experiencing complete restlessness all day, I finally obeyed what I felt was a prompting of the Father—and his answer to the prayer I had prayed as I'd went to sleep the night before. I reached out to her via Facebook Messenger and soon received a response. I shared my experience with her and asked her if I could take her to lunch. She agreed.

Within three days, we sat in front of each other, talking about writing and Jesus. It was great!

As our time together drew to a close, she asked if I would be interested in joining a writing group she belonged to. I was hesitant because I still did not consider myself a writer and did not see myself writing in the future. I thought writing a book would be a one-and-done kind of thing. I'd thought it would be something like, *God, here is the book you wanted me to write. Now, peace out!*

I didn't know what I would have in common with the many women who could write, wanted to write, and probably even loved to read. I was none of those things! I had no aspirations to continue a writing journey. But, God! He always has other plans.

Lynn connected me to Missy Worton, the leader of the writing group 'Warrior Writers'. Missy is also a published author and writing coach. At the time of this writing, I have been a part of Missy's writing group for nearly a year. I learned about different editing and publishing options during my time with her group. However, none of them made me jump within my spirit.

As it would turn out, Missy invites her Warrior Writers to go with her each year to the annual National Religious Broadcasting convention. It just so happened that the convention was in Tennessee that year.

The thought of committing to attend a convention I knew nothing about for a whole week instantly made me anxious, and even more than that, the idea of staying in a house with seventeen other women I did not know (outside of Zoom calls) was panic-worthy in my book. Even though I felt much dread about it all and considered backing out too many times to count, I kept feeling drawn to go. It was as if the Father kept nudging me and saying, *I have something for you there. Trust me.* So, I stepped out in faith, took a enormous leap, and signed up to go.

While in attendance, I had the opportunity to meet many Christian authors and speak with them. One of those authors I met told me about a website that hosts book editors, Reedsy.com. It is funny because I met and spoke with numerous authors that week, yet only one did I inquire about how she found an editor she utilized. I'm glad I took that leap and stepped out of my comfort zone. I am even more glad I asked that author about her editor of choice.

When I returned home after the week of attending the conference, I started my editor search. After a week of prayer and fasting, I felt the Father God was highlighting the ones I should contact for quotes. And through that process, I selected the editor of the book you are now reading. I was so excited to have made that selection. I felt like a new mom on the hunt for a midwife to help me birth a book baby. It was scary! I was prayerful and hopeful, but the unknowns were a bit much, I must say.

Thankfully, God heard my cries for help and united me with an editor who was lovely. She was encouraging and helpful and made the journey easy.

I'm now a published author! I never dreamed of such a turn of events in my life. I can guarantee that none of my English teachers or professors would have either. Praise Jesus for editors! As I have learned, you just have to write, and editors will make it look good. Thank you, Jesus!

My point with this story is that God sometimes calls us

to detour from our life plans. Sometimes, our path along the way is long, challenging, and overwhelming. There are so many people that need to be saved, healed, and delivered, and so little time. For just one person, that can seem like an impossibility. However, what may seem like a small drop in the ocean of life to us very well may end up having a tsunami effect for his kingdom purposes in and through you.

Do you see it? One step of faith by a sweet middle school girl has led to this book being in your hands. I am not sure what was going on in her world or her mind at the time, but I bet she didn't think her invitation would significantly impact so many lives all these years later.

What will you do to advance the kingdom today? Maybe start with something as simple as inviting the person next to you to church on Sunday or ask the person who appears to be struggling in the grocery line if you can pray for them.

> "You never know what the one step you take in faith today may produce in the tomorrow to come"
>
> Cristy Frazier

16

Until Next Time

Thank you again for joining me on this journey and wading into the pool of prayer. I hope you enjoyed your time here with me between the pages. I appreciate you sticking with me as I shared this piece of my heart and my love of prayer. While this mini-book has been no deep-dive, I hope you have experienced a little pep in your prayer step along the way.

Remember, pray without ceasing all your days. The more you do it, the more natural the conversation with the Lord will be. Then, praying aloud and praying for others as the Holy Spirit leads will also become more natural.

Okay, your feet are wet and you have begun floating around in an atmosphere of prayer. It is your turn, now. I pass the prayer torch to you, you mighty prayer warrior. Take your stand (on your knees) and fight the good fight in prayer, for there—and only there—is every spiritual battle won.

Ta-ta for now! I hope to meet you all soon. If not, I will see you all on the other side as we gather at the wedding supper of the Lamb.

Father God Almighty, I thank you for each and every person who read this book. I pray you will be with them and lead them. Please give each of them a heart and a passion for prayer. May their time with you in prayer be fruitful and feed the nations from generation to generation. Please never allow any tear they shed in prayer to be wasted. Instead, please let those tears become the water that nourishes the soil for a bountiful harvest. Please bless them and their families, Lord, and cover them with your love all their days. In Jesus's beautiful name, I pray. Amen!

"Your prayers author your tomorrow"

Cristy Frazier

Appendix A

Prayer Survey

Several years ago, my husband and I led a small group study on prayer. He and I developed the questions below to spur group conversation and self-reflection. The purpose of this survey is to encourage you to take an honest assessment of your prayer life and then reflect on the newfound awareness as you journey through this discussion of prayer. There are no winners or losers. The only wrong answer is a dishonest one. You and God will be the only ones that know the answers.

Take your time and allow the questions to marinate within your mind so that your responses are not just from a place of function and a "get'er done" attitude. Allow the questions to connect with your heart and your soul. Ready, set, go!

1. What does prayer mean to you?
2. How important is prayer to you?
3. Are you satisfied with your prayer life? If not, how would you like your prayer life to change?
4. Do you have daily quiet time(s) or structured time(s) to pray? If not, have you tried to do so in

the past? Do you think it would be beneficial in the future?
5. When is a time you could set aside for prayer?
6. Do you have a specific place (such as a comfy chair or favorite bench at your local park) where you can pray uninterrupted? If not, do you think it would be beneficial? Think of a place you can utilize for your prayer time.
7. Has your prayer life grown over the past few years? If so, how?
8. What, if anything, makes you feel uncomfortable about prayer? Do you find praying to be redundant or boring? Do you lose focus or allow your mind to drift while praying? What could you do to change that?
9. Do you feel connected to God when you pray? Do you "hear" from God? What does that look like or sound like to you? How do you know it is God?
10. Do you have a strategic or systematic prayer plan? Do you keep a list of people to pray for and things to pray about?
11. Do you pray out loud when you are alone? Do you praise and sing aloud to God privately? How would doing so affect your relationship with God and your prayer life?
12. Describe your relationship with God (on a scale of distant to intimate). How has it changed over the past few years?
13. Do you fast? Regularly? How might fasting affect your spiritual growth alongside prayer?
14. Have you ever dedicated an extended block of time specifically for prayer? Alone or with others? If so, what was it like? If not, would it appeal to you?
15. Do you believe there is power in your prayers?

16. Do you feel like your prayers are getting answered? What are some examples?
17. Do you keep a prayer journal? How do you think a prayer journal would be beneficial?
18. Do you pray for people when you say you will? Do you intercede for others without being asked? What are some things in which you pray (or could pray) on behalf of others?
19. Do you feel comfortable praying with (not just for) others about their needs? Do people seek you out to pray for them? Why or why not?
20. Do you pray regularly with your spouse and children? Why or why not?
21. Do you have a prayer partner(s) outside your immediate family? How might having a regular prayer partner help you grow spiritually?
22. Do you ever pray the Scriptures (recite scriptures in prayer)? Which scriptures regarding prayer have been impactful in your life?
23. What does the Bible indicate (through instruction or by example) we should pray about?
24. What hinders your prayers?
25. What does the Bible mention that can hinder our prayers?

Whew! You did it! I highly recommend allowing all these questions and answers to sit and marinate for a few days. Then, come back and revisit the questions and your responses. Please pay attention to how the questions strike you the second time and write additional thoughts that stand out to you from the first to the second time reading through them. Do not stop here with the exploration of prayer! Knowledge only has power when applied. Continue to pray and explore prayer in the days ahead.

Appendix B

An Invitation

Hello, my new friend! What a journey we have been on. I hope you have been encouraged by the Word and ignited in prayer. Before I let you go, I wouldn't feel right without asking, **Will you join us?**

I couldn't go this far with you and let you close this book and walk away without asking. I refuse to walk through those pearly gates with your blood on my hands.

> If I say to the wicked, "You shall surely die," and you give him no warning, nor speak to warn the wicked from his wicked way, in order to save his life, that wicked person shall die for his iniquity, but his blood I will require at your hand. But if you warn the wicked, and he does not turn from his wickedness, or from his wicked way, he shall die for his iniquity, but you will have delivered your soul.
> *Ezekiel 3:18-19*

Did you know Jesus knocks on the door of each of our hearts and calls all of us to him while we are here on earth? **Will you answer his call?**

Once it is our time to transition into eternity, it is his great pleasure to welcome us who are believers through the threshold of the Heavenly doors into our eternal resting place. While on earth, we are allowed to open the door to him. Once we pass, it is his turn to open the door for each of us who call him our Lord. **Will the door be opened to you?**

> Behold, I stand at the door and knock. If anyone hears my voice and opens the door, I will come in to him and eat with him, and he with me.
> *Revelation 3:20*

> ... God our Savior, who desires all people to be saved and to come to the knowledge of the truth.
> *1 Timothy 2:4*

For most of you, I would assume the answer is yes. However, there may still be some who picked up this book because your sweet friend gave it to you, and you wanted to honor them by taking a quick peek. For another, it might be that you have been going through a rough season, you saw the book and decided to check it out because your dear grandmother was a prayer warrior. Maybe you are not a Christian but you just remember that when she prayed, you felt peace and love. Well, no matter the reason, I am glad you did!

If the answer to the question is no, may I have the great pleasure and honor of taking you by the hand and introducing you to my friend Jesus? You, too, can offer your life to him and ask him to be your Lord and Savior. There are no tests and no essays you must write. It is very simple but has generational and eternal blessings and benefits!

It all begins with hearing the gospel (the good news). Romans 10:17 says, "Faith comes from hearing, and hearing through the Word of Christ." To appreciate the good news, you must first acknowledge the bad news. Humanity was created to walk in the presence of God, but we were also created with free will. When Adam and Eve disobeyed the only command they were given in the garden, it resulted in the separation between man and God. Both physical and spiritual deaths entered the story (Genesis 2:16-17). Everyone has followed suit. "All have sinned and fallen short of the glory of God" (Romans 3:23). As a result, we are all subject to the curse of death. "For the wages of sin is death, but the gift of God is eternal life in Christ Jesus our Lord" (Romans 6:23).

But, there is good news! God loves us. He wants us so much so that he gave his son for us so we would have a way back into his presence. "For God so loved the world, that he gave his only Son, that whoever believes in him should not perish but have eternal life" (John 3:16).

He did this for all of us! Everyone! The whole world! All of those who have sinned and fallen short of God's glory. "He is the propitiation for our sins, and not for ours only but also for the sins of the whole world" (1 John 2:2). He does not wait until we are perfect. He meets us exactly where we are with a lifeboat—his Son. "... God shows his love for us in that while we were still sinners, Christ died for us" (Romans 5:8).

So, what do we do? What part do we have in this? How can we be saved? We need to be covered by the blood of Christ. "But now in Christ Jesus, you who once were far off have been brought near by the blood of Christ" (Ephesians 2:13). How do we become saved by being covered by Christ's blood? The simple answer is that we cannot save ourselves. We cannot pay the debt we owe. It is only by grace that we can be saved. Grace, in its simplest form, is unmerited favor. God grants us his favor even though we have not earned it.

But what determines who receives such extraordinary grace? Faith. "For by grace you have been saved through faith. And this is not your own doing; it is the gift of God" (Ephesians 2:8).

What is faith? Is it mere belief that there is a Creator? Is it more? What differentiates faith from mere intellectual acknowledgment is that faith is always accompanied by action. (11)

A quick example of something we may place our faith in would be a parachute. Imagine two people standing at the door of a damaged airplane that is about to crash. Both have a parachute strapped to their back. Both know that parachutes have allowed people to jump from airplanes for years safely. However, one is frozen with fear and stays in the crashing plane while the other jumps and glides safely to Earth. It is evident in this example that while both intellectually believed in the usefulness of a parachute, only one put their faith in it.

Faith requires us to move. It requires us to jump. "And without faith, it is impossible to please him, for whoever would draw near to God must believe that he exists and that he rewards those who seek him" (Hebrews 11:6). People of faith seek God and draw near to him. If you want to know what faith looks like, study Hebrews 11 and the people mentioned in that chapter.

How do we move in faith? Well, that's a process that lasts a lifetime. We do have some instructions to set us on our way. We confess. We confess that we are guilty of sin (1 John 1:9), and we confess our belief in God and the finished work of Jesus on the cross (Romans 10:9-10). We repent of our sins. Repent means to "turn away from sin and dedicate oneself to the amendment of one's life, to feel regret or contrition, to change one's mind." We are baptized. "Repent and be baptized every one of you in the name of Jesus Christ for the forgiveness of your sins, and you will receive the gift of the Holy Spirit" (Acts 2:38). We love one another. "By this, all people will know that you are my disciples if you have a love for one another" (John 13:35).

Finally, we share the good news with others. "Go therefore and make disciples of all nations, baptizing them in the name of the Father and of the Son and of the Holy Spirit, teaching them to observe all that I have commanded you. And behold, I am with you always, to the end of the age" (Matthew 28:19-20).

You may have heard many different opinions and theories on exactly when and how salvation comes. I never encourage one to worry or debate over drawing a definitive line in the sand. None of these things, except for grace, are the things that save you. Remember you cannot earn it. You can only put your faith in it. These are just things that people of faith do.

Want to explore more? I have noted more scriptures below should you wish to dive a little deeper on your own.

We are all sinners and have fallen short.

> All have sinned and fallen short of the glory of God.
> *1 John 1:7-10; Isaiah 64:6;*
> *Romans 3:23-24; Ecclesiastes 7:20*

Because we have sinned and fallen short, we need a Savior.

> For God so loved the world, that he gave his only Son, that whoever believes in him should not perish but have eternal life.
> *John 3:16; Titus 3:5*

All who want eternal life must believe God sent his Son, Jesus, to be the sacrifice in our stead. His blood for ours that we are saved!

> He is the propitiation for our sins, and not for ours only but also for the sins of the whole world.
> *1 John 2:2*

> But now in Christ Jesus you who once were far off
> have been brought near by the blood of Christ.
> *Ephesians 2:13; Ephesians 1:7; John 1:29, 8:24;*
> *Hebrews 9:12, 11:6; Romans 5:9; Leviticus 17:11*

Hear: Hear the Word of God and the message of salvation.

> ... blessed rather are those who hear the word of
> God and keep it!
> *Luke 11:28*

Believe: Believe what you heard as truth and in faith and respond based on that belief.

> For by grace you have been saved through faith.
> And this is not your own doing; it is the gift of God.
> *Ephesians 2:8*

> And without faith it is impossible to please him,
> for whoever would draw near to God must believe
> that he exists and that he rewards those who seek
> him.
> *Hebrews 11:1-40*

Confess: What does it mean to confess one's sins? An act of confessing, especially a disclosure of one's sins in the sacrament of reconciliation, a session for the confessing of sins, going to confession, a statement of what is confessed: such as a written or oral acknowledgment of guilt by a party accused of an offense. (12)

Repent: What does it mean to repent of one's sins? To turn from sin and dedicate oneself to the amendment of one's life, to feel regret or contrition, to change one's mind. (13)

Be baptized: What does it mean to be baptized? The New Testament was written in Greek. If we look up the word 'baptism' in Greek, we find: to dip repeatedly, to immerse, to submerge (of vessels sunk), to cleanse by dipping or submerging, to wash, to make clean with water, to wash oneself, bathe, to overwhelm. (14)

> Repent and be baptized every one of you in the name of Jesus Christ for the forgiveness of your sins, and you will receive the gift of the Holy Spirit.
> *Acts 2:38, 17:30; Romans 10:9-17; Mark 16:16;*
> *1 Peter 1:18-21; Hebrews 10:19-22; John 1:9; 1 John 4:15*

> For by grace you have been saved through faith. And this is not your own doing; it is the gift of God, not a result of works, so that no one may boast.
> *Ephesians 2:8-9*

"Behold, I stand at the door and knock. If anyone hears my voice and opens the door, I will come in to him and eat with him, and he with me" (Revelation 3:20). If you decide to accept the invitation and say yes to Jesus, congratulations and welcome to the eternal family of God Almighty! Go forth and live a life worthy of the blood which was shed for you. Go and replicate what has been done in you for others!

> Go therefore and make disciples of all nations, baptizing them in the name of the Father and of the Son and of the Holy Spirit, teaching them to observe all that I have commanded you. And behold, I am with you always, to the end of the age.
> *Matthew 28:19-20*

> And he said to them, "Go into all the world and proclaim the gospel to the whole creation."
> *Mark 16:15; Matthew 5:14-16*

May it be said of you as you take your last breath here and he welcomes you with a big smile up yonder:

> By Him: His master said to him, "Well done, good and faithful servant. You have been faithful over a little; I will set you over much. Enter into the joy of your master."
>
> *Matthew 25:21, 23*

> By you: I have fought the good fight, I have finished the race, I have kept the faith.
>
> *2 Timothy 4:6-8, 2:5; Philippians 3:12-14; Hebrews 12:1; Acts 20:24; James 1:2*

Tips for a strong finish:

1. **Ask Father God to direct you to a fellowship of believers filled with the Holy Spirit and walking in his truth.**

   Hebrews 10:23-25; Proverbs 27:17

2. **Read the Word daily. As author and pastor, Robby Gallaty, often says, "Get into the Word until the Word gets into you."**

   Deuteronomy 18:17-20; 2 Timothy 3:14-17; Psalm 1, 119:7-11: Acts 17:11

3. **As we have already learned, pray without ceasing!**

   1 Thessalonians 5:17

4. **Live your life unto the Lord, turning away from**

the temptations of sin.

Colossians 3:5-10; John 14:21; 1 Corinthians 10:13; 1 John 3: 6-7; James 4:7

5. Give to others as freely as you have been given.

Luke 6:38

6. Love as you have been loved.

John 13:34

7. Forgive as you have been forgiven.

Matthew 6:14-15

8. Strive to live in peace and harmony with everyone.

Romans 12:16, 18

9. Serve one another.

Galatians 5:13

10. FINISH THE RACE!

Philippians 3:13-14; Hebrews 12:1-2; 2 Timothy 4:7

Appendix C

Behind the Scenes

    Throughout my life, people have often championed me to write a book, but I had no idea where to start or what to write about. It is wild to me that people have seen books within me for years, yet it took me until now to recognize it myself. I would wonder what I have to say that anyone would care to read.

    I bet every writer has had that same thought, and you very well may have yourself. I knew I could write and share things, but I always told myself that others could write and share more purposeful and interesting stories than I ever could. I would allow myself to tune in to the lie that I was merely a reader of stories and not the truth that I could be the writer of my own. Isn't it wild that we are so quick to allow fear, doubt, and absolute lies to become the billboards of our lives instead of the truths of who God created us to be and what he desires us to walk in?

    This book was conceived from my time in prayer. I never would have thought that what the Father has been cultivating in me over the last ten years would turn into a book. Every journal entry, every prayer, and my study on prayer—all carefully planted within me. Planted, watered, and now birthed among these pages for you to read.

When the Father gave me the idea to write *Encouraged & Ignited*, I was a little fear-struck. Not only was I nervous about putting it all together—I was even more nervous about coming up with a title. But, God! As I was processing with the Father in my prayer time, I started asking, "God, what do you want to accomplish with this book? What kingdom impact do you want to achieve by using me as a vessel to pour out among these pages?"

The answer I heard was *'Encouraged & Ignited.'* Isn't God creative? There are so many things we could have answers to if we only asked.

When I was going through my darkest seasons, I looked for encouragement around every corner—just one seed of hope to get me through to the next day. A sweet note from a friend or a song whose words spoke peace into my pain. You get the idea. Until, that is, prayer transformed my heart, mind, and life.

While my soul is no longer restless, my time in prayer is the boost I need when the pressures of life begin to feel overwhelming. Now, I know where to run: the arms of Jesus. Through the building of an intimate prayer life, what was once hope has now become a confidence that when I run to the arms of Jesus, he will welcome me.

Hopefully, the message you found among these pages has been one of encouragement and one that will ignite your prayer life. May you close this book having learned something about prayer. May you be inspired to dive deeper into your own prayer time based on my confessions of hope and a life renewed. Prayer has encouraged and ignited me, and may it be the same for you.

Acknowledgments

First and foremost, I dedicate this book to my Heavenly Father, my precious Lord and Savior, and the sweet Holy Spirit, who lives within me and guides me daily.

A special thanks to my best friend for life and amazing husband of twenty-five years, Chet Frazier. Thank you for getting up and going to work every day in rain, heat, snow, or hail to provide for us so I can stay home and punch this thing out. I am forever grateful for your reading through my book and helping draw the words out of me to bring it to life.

A special shout out to a very special lady and fellow writer, Stephanie Fields, for championing me to write. Out of nowhere, she happened to suggest it to me one day while we were enjoying lunch together. I have no idea what made her think I could or should, but I am so glad she stirred me to triumph over my fears and dive straight in. I look forward to her seeing the finished product. I might not have ever leaped without that seed being planted in my mind by her expression of confidence.

Thank you, Holly, for your excitement and willingness to be the first reader of my work and, technically, my first beta reader. It is unbelievable that most of our friendship over the last ten years has been long-distance, yet I feel closer to you than most I live near and see regularly. Thanks for being my cheerleader and encouraging me to share my writing on social media and showcase it to the world. I love and appreciate you!

Finally, I lay these words upon these pages as a foundation for my daughters and their children to come. May this book be a marker of remembrance in their lives, reminding them that anything is possible with God (see Joshua 4:1-7). May they dive into the deep ends of all their dreams. May they always encourage themselves and others in the Word and be ignited with a passion for the Lord and advancing his kingdom here on earth as in Heaven.

To God be the glory! My cup runneth over!

When all the nation had finished passing over the Jordan, the Lord said to Joshua, "Take twelve men from the people, from each tribe a man, and command them, saying, 'Take twelve stones from here out of the midst of the Jordan, from the very place where the priests' feet stood firmly, and bring them over with you and lay them down in the place where you lodge tonight.'" Then Joshua called the twelve men from the people of Israel, whom he had appointed, a man from each tribe. And Joshua said to them, "Pass on before the ark of the Lord your God into the midst of the Jordan and take up each of you a stone upon his shoulder, according to the number of the tribes of the people of Israel, that this may be a sign among you. When your children ask in time to come, 'What do those stones mean to you?' then you shall tell them that the waters of the Jordan were cut off before the ark of the covenant of the Lord. When it passed over the Jordan, the waters of the Jordan were cut off. So, these stones shall be to the people of Israel a memorial forever."

Joshua 4:1-7

About the Author

Cristy is, first and foremost, a devoted follower of Jesus Christ. Her spiritual journey began early in life but kicked into overdrive in 2013 when it led her to find peace amidst her storms by sitting at the feet of Jesus. Prayer quickly became a staple in her life, and it is evident to anyone who spends time with her that prayer is her refuge and her passion.

Cristy is an entrepreneur at heart and graduated from the Culverhouse School of Business at the University of Alabama. It was there, at univeristy, that she met her husband, Chet. They married shortly after graduating and began moving throughout the Southeastern US as Chet's career led them to five states over the next sixteen years. In 2014, they moved to Tennessee, where they own and operate a communications business. They have settled in a small town just outside of Nashville and are grateful to finally be planting roots.

Cristy and Chet have been blessed with two beautiful daughters, Savanna and Peyton. The Lord has even multiplied their family with two amazing sons-in-law and their first grand-daughter, Sadie. And we cannot forget to mention Cristy and Chet's precious feline rescue—their fur-baby, Luna. She is an addition they did not know they needed, but the Lord knew her love would enrich their lives.

Other than writing, Cristy enjoys time outdoors and near water. Nature is where she feels the most connected to Father God. Having her feet in the sand with the ocean waves tickling her toes is her absolute favorite, but she does not seem to find herself there nearly enough.

Cristy loves time with friends and family, watching movies, listening to worship music (typically very loudly), and—I bet you can guess it—praying. She has a genuine heart, a gift for intercession, and a desire to see all saved, healed, and delivered. She has a passion for prayer and often sits before the Father in confident expectation of praying people right into the Lamb's Book of Life.

For years, she has been a silent warrior for the kingdom, praying prayers of arrows against the forces of darkness. The Lord is drawing her out into the open to share with us how to fill the bowls of Heaven with the sweet incense of our prayers (see Revelation 5:8). May you be blessed by the anointing of her words and the tears poured out over the pages of this book.

> And when he had taken the scroll, the four living creatures and the twenty-four elders fell down before the Lamb, each holding a harp, and golden bowls full of incense, which are the prayers of the saints.
> *Revelation 5:8*

Like What You've Read?

I hope you have enjoyed the journey with me as I shared my thoughts regarding prayer. If so, feel free to stop by my website and share your email so we can stay in touch.

Get to know more about the woman behind the keyboard by visiting my blog or my Facebook page.

 https://cristyfrazier.com/

 https://cristyfrazier.com/?blog=y

 https://facebook.com/cristyfrazier.com/

 https://www.instagram.com/cristyfrazierauthor/

Check out Cristy's other reads on Amazon...

 https://amazon.com/author/cristyfrazier

 Scan the QR code below for quick access to it all

#prayersarepowerful

Notes

We, as Followers of The Way, are Instructed to Pray:
1. https://godgiftsyou.com/blog/2019/3/13/calling-and-purpose-8barnabas-and-exhortation#:

Avenues of Prayer:
2. Thanksgiving:
https://www.google.com/search?q=Thanksgiving+defined&oq=Thanksgiving+defined&gs_lcrp=
3. Praise:
https://www.google.com/search?q=praise+defined&sca_esv=
4. Confession:
https://www.google.com/search?q=confession+defined&sca_esv=
5. Supplication:
https://www.google.com/search?q=supplication+defined&sca_esv=

My Foundational Prayers:
6. Armor image: Illustration, Mallory Humphries
7. Police image: Illustration, Mallory Humphries
8. Iron Dome Defense System: https://en.wikipedia.org/wiki/Iron_Dome#:

Jesus and Prayer:
9. Supplication:
https://Biblehub.com/dictionary/s/supplication.htm
10. Intercession:
https://www.merriam-webster.com/dictionary/intercession

Appendix B: An Invitation:
11. Long Hollow, "The Great Invitation," 33:06 and 33:27. 18, March 2024, https://www.youtube.com/watch?v=w2rEql8SjKw&t=101s
12. Confession: https://www.merriam-webster.com/dictionary/confession
13. Repent: https://www.merriam-webster.com/dictionary/repent
14. Baptism: https://www.Biblestudytools.com/lexicons/greek/nas/baptizo.html

www.ingramcontent.com/pod-product-compliance
Lightning Source LLC
Chambersburg PA
CBHW031411040426
42444CB00005B/518